THE
TALENT
JOURNEY

THE 55-MINUTE GUIDE TO
EMPLOYEE COMMUNICATIONS
BY **KEVIN KEOHANE**

W0006592

FIRST PUBLISHED IN 2010 BY
VERB PUBLISHING LTD
THE COW SHED, HYDE HALL FARM,
BUCKLAND, HERTS SG9 0RU,
UNITED KINGDOM

ISBN 978-0-95646-721-8

TO MY DAD, WHO TAUGHT ME
THE POWER OF LISTENING

WHAT'S INSIDE

1. WHAT THIS BOOK'S ABOUT   1

2. BUSINESS CASES FOR PEOPLE COMMUNICATIONS   7

3. BIG CHANGES IN AUDIENCES AND MEDIA   11

4. STAKEHOLDERS   17

5. AUDIENCES   21

      SCHOOL LEAVERS, GRADUATES, EXPERIENCED HIRES   23

      LEADERS   27

      FUNCTIONAL HEADS   31

      LINE MANAGERS   35

      EMPLOYEES   37

6. THE TALENT JOURNEY   43

      BRAND AND TALENT   49

      EMPLOYER BRAND & EMPLOYEE VALUE PROPOSITION   51

      RECRUITMENT COMMUNICATION   53

      ON-BOARDING, INDUCTION & FIRST 90 DAYS   57

      EMPLOYEE ENGAGEMENT   59

            HR AND CAREER DEVELOPMENT EXPERIENCE   63

            BRAND ENGAGEMENT EXPERIENCE   67

            CHANGE EXPERIENCE   69

            DEPARTURE EXPERIENCE   73

7. THE THREE M'S   77

      MESSAGES   79

      MEDIA   83

      MEASUREMENT   85

8. DEFINITION OF TERMS   88

9. AFTERWORD   96

On facing pages you'll find a summary of core thoughts and ideas. Try adding them to presentations or the bottom of your emails and see if you can start a conversation.

1. WHAT THIS BOOK'S ABOUT

This book is intended to be the zero-BS guide to communicating with people before, during and after their association with your organisation as employees – THE TALENT JOURNEY. It's written for anyone, from CEO to a junior designer in an agency, who wants a quick and dirty overview of the whole thing in bite-sized pieces.

Edward De Bono outlines ten SIMPLICITY PRINCIPLES. They're a great guide to getting many things right. Most books on employee communication and employee engagement (whether on the topic of brand, leadership, HR or change) ignore them:

→   Put a high value on simplicity

→   Be determined to seek simplicity

→   Understand the matter very well

→   Design alternatives

→   Challenge and discard existing elements

→   Be prepared to start over again

→   Use concepts

→   Break things down into smaller units

→   Be prepared to trade off other values for simplicity

→   Know for whose sake the simplicity is being designed

The goal of this book is simple – to give you some powerful ideas to help you answer the questions that really matter when it comes to employee communications.

This book was inspired in part by Marty Neumeier's THE BRAND GAP and ZAG , which tackled the massively complex yet blindingly obvious world of innovation and branding. (He's a lot better at it than I am, but we both seem to adhere to the same principles.)

In summary, then, if the topic can't be covered in two pages, it hasn't met the criteria. Purists and my fellow "experts" might be righteously indignant at my shorthand. The intention here is simple: MORE INSIGHT GAINED PER MINUTE than you'll get from longer books and expensive conferences.

HOW IT'S STRUCTURED

First, we'll look at some BIG PICTURE stuff like why organisations should bother to do any of this stuff at all, and social and media trends. This leads us to a discussion about stakeholders and audiences. STAKEHOLDERS, who are people who have an interest in what you and your people SAY AND DO as an organisation. AUDIENCES, because they must sit at the heart of everything you do in employee communication.

Second, we'll look at something called the EMPLOYEE LIFECYCLE. If you Google it you'll find more than you ever needed to know about it. It's not a new idea, but it's probably the simplest way to think about why, how and when to engage with employee audiences.

Think of this book and its ideas as a camp knife with all sorts of tools. Each bit does something different, but it's all part of something bigger.

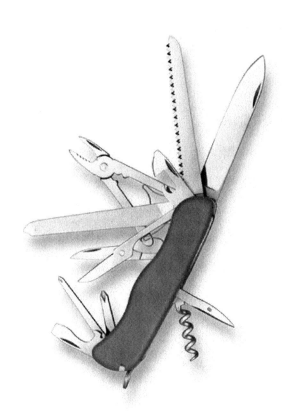

In short, it's breaking a person's entire relationship with your organisation into chronological chunks — BEFORE, DURING and AFTER they work with you.

Third, we'll explore the Three Ms of MESSAGES, MEDIA and MEASUREMENT. These are the important building blocks of communication with employees — and it's this that most other books spend most of their time gasbagging about — but they don't deliver value unless you get the other stuff first.

The value of employee engagement ought to be self-evident. Unfortunately, more money's been spent on determining the value of employee communications than on actually doing it.

2. BUSINESS CASES FOR PEOPLE COMMUNICATIONS

WHY BOTHER?

Ten or fifteen years ago the big debate was about "How can you prove that people communications makes a difference to how the business performs?" (Probably one of the most stupid and lengthy debates ever held. But apparently it needed to happen in a world where "What gets measured gets managed". Sort of like calculating the ROI of your telephone system.)

A whole industry grew out of this, prompted by a 1997 article in the *Harvard Business Review* about Sears and something called THE SERVICE-PROFIT CHAIN. In summary, if you hire good people and treat them well (and they do their jobs well), then they treat your customers well. And wow: people spend more time and money with your organisation.

BUSINESS BENEFITS

There are masses of statistically valid global studies from respectable, credible organisations that make the case. There are also loads of pseudo-scientific, quasi-financial assertions. In time, you'll be able to spot the difference.

Attraction + engagement = $$$.

Some of the key business benefits of getting employee engagement right include:

→ TOTAL SHAREHOLDER RETURN and EARNINGS PER SHARE tend to be higher in organisations with engaged employees compared to those with disengaged employees.

→ Corporate/Consumer BRAND EQUITY and CUSTOMER LOYALTY are higher in organisations with engaged employees.

→ ATTRACTION, PERFORMANCE and RETENTION of high performance employees is higher in organisations with engaged workforces.

→ The cost of RECRUITING and RETAINING talent is lower in organisations with engaged employees.

Online social and professional networks, channel fragmentation and reduced trust in media have changed the rules of the game. Some companies still haven't noticed.

3. BIG CHANGES IN AUDIENCES AND MEDIA

Twenty-five years ago, an organisation could reach nearly every household in the land by advertising on three television channels and in fewer than ten mainstream media publications. It was similar inside organisations with bulletin boards and printed newsletters.

Things are very different today.

There are three basic concepts here that apply to the world of employee communications:

→ THE RISE OF NETWORKS – largely (but not solely) driven by technology, the expansion, ease of use and access to individual personal and professional networks means that traditional approaches to communication with people (whether inside or outside your organisation) have changed profoundly.

PEOPLE HAVE ACCESS TO FAR MORE MEDIA CHANNELS AND INFORMATION SOURCES THAN YOU CAN POSSIBLY CONTROL.

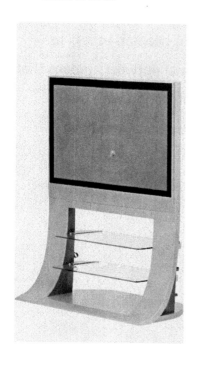

SO STOP KIDDING YOURSELF
ABOUT CONTROLLING IT.

JUST BE PRESENT IN THE
CONVERSATION.

AND BE HONEST.

It's now very easy for (your) people to check up on you. So be present in the conversation – and be honest.

→ FRAGMENTATION OF MEDIA – also largely (but not solely) driven by technology, it is cheaper and easier than ever to communicate, and media have fragmented. CONTENT has been separated from the MEANS OF DISTRIBUTION.

→ DIMINISHING TRUST IN MEDIA – numerous social and commercial studies demonstrate that people no longer trust traditional media such as advertising and mainstream publications; they tend to trust friends and people like themselves.

The result of this is that people have a lot more access and choice. Employees and stakeholders are no longer captive audiences.

Individual stakeholder groups don't exist in isolation. In fact, any individual may occupy more than one group at any given time. It's important to look at it as a system.

4. STAKEHOLDERS

Every organisation has numerous third parties who have some interest or stake in what the organisation does.

This includes government regulators, quasi-governmental organisations, the investment and financial community, suppliers, competitors (for business and for talent), special interest groups, trade unions, partners, current employees, past employees, future employees... and so on.

Until relatively recently, all of these stakeholders tended to be CAPTIVELY MANAGED – that is, specific functional owners in the organisation were responsible for relationships with these stakeholders. Corporate Communications dealt with the media and investors; HR and legal with unions, and so on.

However, due to the social and technology issues raised in Section 3, it really doesn't work this way anymore (though some businesses prefer to pretend it does and continue to organise themselves, and behave, accordingly).

Although these stakeholders have always overlapped, with the fragmentation of media and proliferation of information and communication technologies, the overlap is far more transparent than before. So your supplier, or that government agency, may be a partner, an investor and a competitor all at

Left hand, meet right hand. Now, shake.

STAKEHOLDER	EXAMPLES OF INTERESTS
Owners/Shareholders	Profit, performance, direction, sustainability
Government	Taxation, legislation, low unemployment
Senior management	Staff performance, targets, growth
Non-managerial staff	Rates of pay, job security
Trade Unions	Working conditions, minimum wage, legal requirements
Customers	Value, quality, customer care, ethical products
Creditors	Credit score, new contracts, liquidity
Local community	Jobs, involvement, environmental issues

SOURCE: ADAPTED FROM WIKIPEDIA

the same time. This means that what you are saying to them on one page, or screen or conversation, needs to be JOINED UP. Saying one thing to an investor and something totally different to a supplier, when they are one and the same, makes you look like a complete idiot. And it's a WASTE OF TIME AND MONEY.

STAKEHOLDER ANALYSIS

So it's really important for anyone involved in internal and/or external communications about your organisation to have been a part of conducting a pretty robust STAKEHOLDER ANALYSIS.

Basically, this means making a list of all the different people who have an interest in your organisation, and then making a list of their position, attitudes, attributes, and impact (see table, opposite).

Then, you can spot overlaps, opportunities to engage more effectively and clearly, and by and large do a better job at joining up communications – not just internally. This then helps you ALIGN YOUR MESSAGING as well as your MEDIA a lot better.

The single most important insight you can have about your employees: what gets people out of bed in the morning.

5. AUDIENCES

You'd be surprised how many books about employee communications say a lot about theory, communication channels (media) and content... and very little about EMPLOYEES.

You know, human resources. HUMAN BEINGS, with whom you are seeking to engage. Those things we call "our most valuable asset" in every single annual review printed today.

If you forget your AUDIENCE, and if your AUDIENCE – their desires, needs and preferences – are not at the heart of everything you communicate, you might as well pack up and go home. It's time to ask the hard (easy) questions, like:

→ Do we really know what gets people out of bed in the morning?

→ Do we know who people trust, where and to whom they turn to for the most up-to-date information?

HINT: It's probably not your intranet, your wiki, your newsletter or your next staff presentation.

Data is fine, but what makes it useful is what you do with it. It's insight and judgement that matter (which can exist without data). So be prepared to trust your gut.

It's important to have intelligence about your AUDIENCE – things you know, things you can assume, things you don't know, things about similar audiences in similar situations. While Section 7 talks more about MEASUREMENT, it's important to note that AUDIENCE INTELLIGENCE isn't just about employee surveys and focus groups. It's OK to follow instincts and experience as well.

SCHOOL LEAVERS, GRADUATES AND EXPERIENCED HIRES

How do you hire the best people who will deliver great results?

There is no one size fits all solution, because these audiences are at DIFFERENT LIFE STAGES and have DIFFERENT NEEDS, requirements and priorities. There are also cultural factors that can have a tremendous impact; what South Americans seek in their careers is different from Europeans. We also now have three generations (soon to be four) in our workplaces, and while GENERATIONAL THEORY has its limitations (it's a step away from astrology), it's still something we need to take into account.

With SCHOOL LEAVERS and GRADUATES, what appeals is likely to be a combination of things: egalitarian culture, prestige, rapid career development, work-life balance, and "meaningful" work. With EXPERIENCED HIRES, it's likely to be seeing the results of their work and providing challenges and opportunities for personal development.

What motivates somebody to join your organisation isn't necessarily what will motivate them to stay.

People's needs and ambitions change over time, so you'll need to take that into account.

Most research says the same thing. What people seek is:

→ Following their passion,

→ Doing interesting work,

→ Working with interesting people,

→ Getting recognition, and

→ Being rewarded.

If you are in a sector that is perceived as less sexy (say, retail) you'll need to work hard to ensure that what you say brings to life what is, in reality, a challenging, fast-paced career where sharp people move ahead quickly. Many of the people who might thrive in your organisation might NEVER CONSIDER WORKING IN IT; find out who and where they are.

Remember too what we talked about earlier – these people are human beings who consume a variety of media to find out information about you and your organisation.

So don't just rely on your careers site (although it is critically important), or job boards, or recruitment agencies. You'll need to make sure you're working PR channels, social media, word of mouth and other ways of enhancing your reputation as a place to work for all these audiences. Hiring head hunters, agencies and recruitment advertising might not be the only solution, either.

Leaders are interested in delivering results. Not only improvements in business performance (objective), but also in how they are perceived (subjective/personal).

Make sure that they can see how effective communication delivers both.

LEADERS

Clearly, leaders are a critical audience. They are often the public face of the organisation externally. Internally, they set the tone in terms of attitude, performance and behaviour for the entire organisation. It's a cliché, but a good one – great leaders WALK THE TALK.

While it's often assumed that good communication skills are a requirement to progress from management to leadership, in reality this is often not the case. (Some very successful leaders are appallingly poor communicators, usually because of this very assumption).

Leaders need to be equipped to perform their employee communication roles, just as they need to be equipped to perform their many other roles (including external communication).

→ MAKE THE CASE – critical to success with this audience is, of course, making the case (see Section 2 for the top line). It's essential to ensure that leaders see employee communication as a value-creating INVESTMENT, and not an optional expense. Be sure you are always equipped with the facts and data you need to support your communication efforts.

Employee communication is about value creation both by and for employees. Once leaders get this, you better put on your track shoes.

→ EDUCATE AND ENGAGE – another key approach is to ensure that leaders are engaged in CRAFTING THE COMMUNICATIONS within the organisation. Given most leaders' limited time, this can be extremely challenging. On the other hand, great leaders in some leading organisations typically dedicate 20 percent of their time (one day per week) to internal and employee communications.

→ GET UPSTREAM – communication and engagement strategy can help shape and improve business, HR, change, and brand performance. The further downstream communicators are, the less likely they'll be able to make an impact. This ensures COMMUNICATION CREATES VALUE for the business, and doesn't just move information around.

→ SYSTEMS THINKING – conventional wisdom seems to suggest specialisation and a competence-driven approach to employee communications is essential. Nothing could be further from the truth. The emergence and gathering momentum of DESIGN THINKING amply demonstrates that every other strategic and creative profession is moving in exactly the opposite direction.

We have entered an age of multi-specialism that has reduced the traditional technical skills of professional communicators to a hygiene factor.

An increasingly complex and fast-moving world poses leadership challenges that deep functional communication expertise alone is ill-equipped to deal with.

You need to be able to join the dots.

In an increasingly complex, diverse, and unstable world, what counts is the ability to JOIN THE DOTS. It's not about becoming incrementally better at things you already do. It is about trying new approaches and employing a wider range of problem solving skills with reference to THE WHOLE SYSTEM – not just the microcosm called internal communications.

So, while it has become a truism that leaders must walk the talk and practice what they preach, what is equally important is that they buy into and not only understand, but ACTIVELY DEMONSTRATE AND CHAMPION, your engagement effort.

If your leaders are saying one thing and doing another, your engagement effort will suffer.

FUNCTIONAL HEADS

Few books on the topic address the importance of a key management and leadership group – functional leaders. Whether finance, marketing, HR, IT, facilities, corporate communications, while these people are "leaders" and "managers" they also need special consideration regarding their patch of turf.

It's important to make sure that any communication with employees past, present and future takes into account what the input, effect and likely output might be on DIFFERENT PARTS OF

Lyndon Johnson said it best: "It's better to have them on the inside of the tent pissing out than on the outside of the tent pissing in."

Even if it doesn't go perfectly, there will be a lot less mess to clean up if you've worked across silos. (Plus, leaders love it when people consult each other without being told to.)

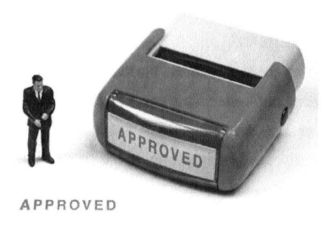

APPROVED

THE ORGANISATION. Since organisations are complex systems, it can be hard to precisely predict outcomes, but doing a bit of homework and engaging with the wider functional network is often the difference between success and embarrassment.

→ DON'T ASSUME THEY AREN'T AFFECTED – it's possible that what you plan to communicate about brand, HR, change or whatever, might have an impact on what the function is doing. It could be as simple as timing things to avoid information overload, or as complicated as re-thinking your approach based on valuable input from functional leads.

→ EDUCATE AND ENGAGE – it never hurts to involve people in other Kingdoms to share ideas, approaches and information. You might learn something, and they might learn something (or even flatter you and steal your ideas).

→ SCORE POINTS – leadership loves it when people consult each other without being told to.

It seems blindingly obvious, but important programmes can fail before launch because someone in a remote part of the organisation wasn't involved or consulted. Just ask.

Who is best placed to connect organisational and individual goals?

Line managers.

Who is least empowered, equipped and rewarded for communicating well?

Hmm...

LINE MANAGERS

Clearly, line managers are a critical audience, too. They are often (though not always) THE MOST TRUSTED SOURCE OF INFORMATION to employees about the organisation and what is happening in it.

Like leaders, line managers need to be equipped to perform their employee communication and engagement role – from attraction and recruitment, through to career development and managing exits effectively.

In high-performing organisations, line managers are typically equipped with regular training and materials to help them fulfil their role as key communicators and culture carriers within the organisation.

→ MAKE IT EASY – time-starved line managers know they need to communicate; often they don't know what, when, why and how. Make it easy by providing consistent, credible, easy to use materials and content.

→ EMPOWER FACE-TO-FACE APPROACHES – line managers have the most face-to-face opportunities with employees, so make the maximum possible use of this approach with this audience.

Equip, empower, recognise and reward good communication by managers.

→ JOIN IT UP – help line managers understand, and equip them to articulate, how different strands in the organisation's strategy, from brand to vision to change to HR, fit into their day-to-day jobs. If they get it, chances are their people will also get it.

Most current communication research demonstrates that the most important and trusted communicator to employees is the line manager. Engagement efforts should include this group not only as an audience to inform, but a group to EQUIP AND EMPOWER with the tools to ensure employees can make the engagement effort relevant to their part of the business and their day-to-day jobs.

EMPLOYEES

Guess what? Yes, employees are a critical audience, too. (One would hope so in a book about employee communications).

Getting employee communication right is part art and part science. It's easy to do it very badly. With painstaking effort, it can be done in a depressingly average way.

It's also easy to do it really well. But it still takes effort. If you remember what gets people out of bed in the morning, you're half way there.

Do yourself a favour: forget push vs. pull, top-down vs. bottom-up vs. peer-to-peer models of communication.

What should you be doing? All of them.

Someone once said, "People want to do a good job. They don't go to work to be disengaged and have a bad attitude. That's something we do to them, day after day, in the way me manage them and communicate with them."

A lot of lip service is given to "two-way communication" versus "top-down" communication versus "bottom-up" communication. Guess what? All three are needed. If we believe the business cases from Section 2, and have any insights from Sections 3 and 4, then:

→   How employees interact with EACH OTHER and with YOUR STAKEHOLDERS has a massive impact on the performance of your organisation.

→   How you engage and communicate effectively with employees is driven by THEIR NEEDS, not YOUR NEEDS.

→   IT'S NEVER BEEN EASIER to talk with employees and get them talking.

Employees want to do a good job. It's usually a matter of making sure you are getting the right information to them in the right way at the right time.

This means thinking about what's important to them, not what's important to you.

Most research in employee engagement indicates that at any given time, only about 1/3 of employees are actively "engaged" in their jobs and their organisations.

The remaining 2/3 are either not actively engaged, or worse, could even be actively pissed off at you and say mean things to their friends about you whenever they can. Not good for your reputation.

Making sure that the engagement effort provides a clear and compelling case is important, but equally important is making sure that employees understand what the effort means to the organisation, their part of the organisation, their team and their own role on a very real, day to day basis. It's also about what is provided in return, too.

Engaging people happens within a complex system. A change in one part of the system has knock on effects on other parts.

Join things up! (Did I say that already?)

6. THE TALENT JOURNEY

What a lot of businesses don't realise is that employee communication starts BEFORE PEOPLE JOIN THEM and continues AFTER THEY LEAVE.

In an "audience-driven" environment where "media neutrality" and "integrated communications" are bandied about with feral abandon, and "multi-specialist" skills are increasingly seen to add value, it's easy to feel a bit queasy floating around in an alphabet soup of jargon.

What people are really trying to say is that with all that fragmentation taking place, the proliferation of media, overlapping audiences, and increasingly complex stakeholder management and operational environments: JOIN THINGS UP.

When you look at the entire employee experience and the disciplines that match this journey, it's clear that while specialism in any one part of the journey is important, it's just as important (if not more) to be able to see the LINKS AND RELATIONSHIPS amongst these stages.

Engaging people happens within a complex system. A change in one part of the system has knock on effects on other parts. This is why many engagement, change and HR process changes fail to deliver the results intended. They plug a hole in

Less is often more. People can only process about three things at a time.

So pick a peg to hang your hat on.

one part of the boat but cause a leak somewhere else. In other words, now more than ever is the time to JOIN THINGS UP.

Marketing, stop sending marketing messages to employees who are also getting HR messages from HR; vision and strategy messages from the C-suite; change communications from the management-consultant-infestation calling itself the "Programme Management Office"; and a raft of other internal communications that require serious AIR TRAFFIC CONTROL to manage the employee engagement space.

This is just too much information for people to take aboard. There is a condition that is well on its way to entering the medical lexicon: INFORMATION FATIGUE SYNDROME.

Here's a tip from the world of psychology: the human mind can simultaneously hold no more than three (plus or minus two) things. You need to pick a peg to hang your hat on.

Create a cohesive core idea and a flexible framework for your communications. Whether this is your BIG HAIRY AUDACIOUS GOAL, or your VISION, or your VALUES, or your STRATEGY, or your AGENDA FOR CHANGE, make sure that whatever you communicate, to any audience, can draw a "red thread" or line-of-sight back to it.

THE TALENT JOURNEY

What is the entire experience a person has before, during and after their association with your organisation?

Is it all lined up, or is it a bit of a mish-mash?

| BRAND EXPERIENCE | EMPLOYER BRAND & EMPLOYEE VALUE PROPOSITION (EVP) | RECRUITMENT EXPERIENCE |

Also remember, it is a journey, and often a long one.

A big launch and no follow-up will fail.
Ongoing, planned, incremental effort works.

ON-BOARDING,	HR & CAREER	DEPARTURE
INDUCTION &	DEVELOPMENT	EXPERIENCE
FIRST 90 DAYS	EXPERIENCE	
		(NOTE — MAY
	BRAND	RETURN TO
	ENGAGEMENT	START)
	EXPERIENCE	
	CHANGE	
	EXPERIENCE	

Your brand isn't owned only by the marketing department. In fact, it isn't even owned by your organisation. It only exists in the minds of your stakeholders.

So maybe your employees (the people who actually serve your customers/clients) might have something to do with it?

BRAND AND TALENT

The first thing people will encounter is your brand – YOUR REPUTATION as a company. This encompasses everything – your advertising, your products and services, your PR, your buildings, and what people inside and outside the organisation say about you.

It should be TRUE, INTERESTING and DIFFERENTIATE you from your business competitors.

And your reputation as a company isn't entirely managed by your marketing, advertising, corporate communications and PR efforts. Your reputation is WHAT OTHER PEOPLE THINK IT IS, not what you say it is.

People have become much more sophisticated media users as channels have proliferated. They not only consume media, they produce it. The touch points have become more numerous and both you and your audience have much GREATER CHOICE AND GREATER VOICE.

The best organisations find that their corporate/consumer brand incorporates some element of reputation as an employer. Unprompted questions about the brand should include something about "...AND PEOPLE LOVE WORKING THERE."

So while it might not always seem that marketing plays a role in employee engagement, you might want to think again. And marketing might want to talk to HR about it.

The same rules apply to your employer brand as to your corporate/consumer brands.

What makes you different, why is that relevant to the best employees, and how authentic is it as a reflection of the employee experience?

EMPLOYER BRAND AND EMPLOYEE VALUE PROPOSITION

The next thing our audiences encounter is your employer brand – your reputation as a place to work.

Your corporate reputation is the overall ASSET that will help determine whether people consider, try and are loyal to your product or service. The employer brand does much the same thing for future and current employees.

Your reputation as an employer isn't entirely managed through your employer value proposition (what you put forward as the employment "deal" on offer), your recruitment advertising and your careers site.

Like corporate brand, it crosses many boundaries including your online footprint, your on and offline PR and media relations activities, your relationships with recruitment agencies and channels, and of course word of mouth. It also covers internal communications, employee referral, HR and change communications.

It has to be TRUE, DISTINCTIVE, and it has to DIFFERENTIATE you from your COMPETITORS FOR TALENT (who are not always your business competitors). It shouldn't be SOMETHING FOR EVERYONE. You need to find what makes you special and stick to that core idea, RELENTLESSLY.

To what extent does your reputation as a business need to align with your reputation as an employer? Usually, but not always, quite a lot.

The degree to which your employer brand aligns to your corporate brand depends. The more equity you have with your audience in your corporate brand, the more latitude you have with expressing your employer brand.

So for example, if you are one of the world's leading consumer brands, it might actually be a problem for your reputation as an employer. You can be smothered by people's love for your product or service, which may have little to do with THE WORK IT TAKES TO DELIVER IT.

But there is no hard and fast rule.

RECRUITMENT COMMUNICATION

So, a person has thought about your reputation as a company and has started to form an opinion about your reputation and attractiveness as an employer.

The next step is ensuring that the candidates who are perfect matches for your requirements engage with your attraction and recruitment system – and that those who aren't, don't (whisper it quietly, but this is EVERY BIT AS IMPORTANT.)

It's essential that your core assets deliver well – your employee referral approach, your recruitment agency relationships, your recruitment advertising and careers site. And it's equally important that your other assets aren't

What is the experience you create for the talent you need to hire?

The selection and recruitment process is as much as who you say no to (and how you manage it) as it is about who you say yes to.

forgotten – namely social media and PR approaches. This means that every communication in your marketplace for talent should explicitly align with your EMPLOYEE VALUE PROPOSITION. CONSISTENCY, CLARITY and COMPELLING CREDIBILITY are the name of the game.

A big no-no is different parts of the organisation recruiting with completely different messages, tone of voice, look and feel – especially when these ads appear on the same page (by accident).

The transition from "recruitment" to "engagement" is an interesting one. Engagement should begin BEFORE THE JOB IS OFFERED, since the experience a person has throughout this process is critical. In addition, things like new joiner extranets or more engaging pre-joining processes can pay significant dividends in terms of productivity and connection to the organisation.

Also, be careful with all those people YOU SAY NO TO. Some companies create 1,000 brand assassins a day by being rude to people who applied for a job, or treating them like a number. More often than not, they are a consumer. (This applies to your agencies, too; sometimes their behaviour toward candidates can be genuinely appalling.)

Get off to the right start. What's more important – to get things done quickly, or to get them done right?

This is a window into the culture of your organisation. Open it. Have a look. Does short-termism start here?

ONBOARDING, INDUCTION AND FIRST 90 DAYS

To quote another cliché, "You never get a second chance to make a first impression."

Broadly speaking, 20% of employee turnover will take place in the FIRST SIX MONTHS. It's all too easy to let the new hire disappear into their new role without the right amount of real connection to who you are as an organisation and what their connection to you means.

And all those wonderful differentiating promises you made in your employee value proposition FLY OUT THE WINDOW.

It's amazing how poorly even large, successful, global organisations manage this. There is a FALSE ECONOMY in getting people "in place" before they are truly prepared to take on their role. It's easy to lose one, two, three or even six months of productivity as people find their feet. If you make the right hires, this helps people HIT THE GROUND RUNNING. If you deliver on your promises, you won't have to go BACK TO SQUARE ONE and spend time and money recruiting for the job again.

And make sure it's not just about health, safety, environment, operational processes and filling out forms. Get people CONNECTED to the brand and what the business does. Not long presentations, but interactive exercises with other people.

Engagement doesn't happen in isolation.

It's the result of systems thinking applied to communication and behaviour, consistently and over time, by design.

Smart companies start doing this before the person even starts – for example, a "new joiners" extranet where people can fill out forms and interact with other new joiners and future colleagues.

Make sure every role has a clear first 90-days plan. You might even plan the first two weeks day by day.

EMPLOYEE ENGAGEMENT

How can EMPLOYEE ENGAGEMENT be a mere subhead in a book on employee communications? The answer's simple: because it is merely PART OF A LARGER AND MORE COMPLEX SYSTEM.

There has recently been a general realisation that no SINGLE PART of the organisation actually owns the employee engagement agenda.

The best engagement efforts generally involve a cross-functional team from ACROSS THE BUSINESS. Accountability for the engagement agenda is shared across key functions – human resources, internal communications, organisational development, information technology, marketing, change management, corporate communications and the leadership/strategy team.

JOIN THINGS UP!

If one function believes it is the sole owner of the employee engagement agenda, ENGAGEMENT SUFFERS:

→ Efforts come from only one functional perspective, so they are NOT INTEGRATED AND ALIGNED and address only part of the issue

→ Efforts have less BUY-IN AND COMMITMENT from other parts of the organisation

→ Efforts have less impact since they have FEWER RESOURCES deployed from a single function

→ Efforts are inefficient as different functions pursue DIFFERENT APPROACHES AND OBJECTIVES

This is where it can all get quite complicated – and potentially political. There are A NUMBER OF CORE DRIVERS you can select to form the main focus of the effort. These include your vision, mission, values, commercial business strategy, customers/clients, people agenda, leadership style, corporate responsibility agenda, brand and many more.

Many practitioners have a deep belief in the supremacy of one or more of these potential central drivers – naturally biased towards THE PERSPECTIVE FROM WHICH THEY VIEW THINGS. It's probable that HR professionals will see the natural centre of

Does your HR communication take into account what gets people out of bed in the morning?

Or does it read like the instruction manual for a digital camera?

gravity in the human capital corner, while marketing may well believe it's all about living the brand, and change managers expect it to be about getting people connected to workstreams.

HR AND CAREER DEVELOPMENT EXPERIENCE

Human Resources communications are generally about a range of things, from the risk management of employee litigation at one extreme, to creating a happy and healthy working environment at the other.

With no disrespect to HR practitioners and the consultants who help them communicate, the content can sometimes be pretty dry and dreary and, well, INHUMAN. It's often POORLY CONNECTED to brand and strategy. And it sometimes focuses too much on the delivery approach, not THE OUTCOME.

I blame the lawyers, mainly.

But HR and organisational development communication has come a long way. Transactional intranet sites and engaging face to face sessions beat the heck out of printed policy manuals.

What's important to keep in mind here is that it's very, very easy to get so close to the minutiae of HR practice and policies that you forget WHY YOU EMPLOYED PEOPLE IN THE FIRST PLACE.

How can you make HR communication sexier?

Make it bigger. Make it about results, personal growth and your Big Hairy Audacious Goals. Because, actually, it is.

Remember that your people are your brand, so your HR communications – not just in terms of design and tone, but in terms of messaging and context – must exude your brand and your employee value proposition from every seam.

Better still, your operational HR practices and processes should too. It's no good claiming "straightforward" as a corporate value and then deploying a performance planning and career development process that requires a Ph.D. in Human Resources to unwind.

Whatever it's about – reward, benefits, recognition, performance planning, training and development, discipline, health and safety, you name it – every HR communication and process needs to be lined up with your business strategy, brand, vision and/or values.

Remember the peg you picked earlier in Section 6? HANG HR'S HAT ON IT.

Brand engagement = every employee knowing their impact on the customer experience, and why that matters.

And then being able to do something about it. Authentically.

BRAND ENGAGEMENT EXPERIENCE

You've invested in your brand. Sales and marketing are firing on all cylinders. Leaders, line managers and HR have lined up everyone in the same strategic direction. The product is superb and at the right price. Even your retail and work environments are oozing your Core Purpose. In short, you are ready to sit back and watch the money roll in.

And then, YOUR CUSTOMERS MEET YOUR PEOPLE.

Whether they work the shop floor, run the back or middle office, provide advice, pick up the phone or lick envelopes, does every one of your employees UNDERSTAND YOUR BRAND?

Do they know what it stands for? Why it stands for what it does in relation to competitors? What they can do and whether that BUILDS or DAMAGES the brand?

This is BRAND ENGAGEMENT. Making sure that everyone, or at least those who have the most important contact with the people who ultimately pay the bills, are DOING what the brand is SAYING. This means leaders walk the talk and can give the right answer to questions. Line managers understand the brand and are equipped to help their people apply it to their day-to-day jobs in meaningful ways. Employees do the right thing and are given the tools and information to do so.

If you've understood the system and thought through all the parts of the talent journey, brand engagement is actually quite easy.

If everyone's working in silos, you'll need to work a lot harder at it.

Does this mean you create an army of BRANDWASHED CLONES? It won't if you're smart about the way you communicate your values. It won't if you've done the earlier stuff right and joined up your thinking – if you've got your EVP right and you've recruited the right people in the first place. When you've done this right, "on-brand" behaviour is already second nature. No shoe-horns required.

But it does mean YOU NEED TO DO SOMETHING to make sure your people are enhancing one of your biggest assets every day, and do it on an ongoing basis.

CHANGE EXPERIENCE

"Yep," the Old Tymer said, rocking back in his chair with all two teeth clenched on a ragged corn-cob pipe. "The only thing constant is change."

Change, often rapid, large scale and unexpected, is a given in today's business environment. Managing change is probably a CONTRADICTION IN TERMS. And given the complex systems that are today's organisations, it can be nearly impossible to predict or map what a change in one area of the environment is going to have on other areas of the system.

The number one reason change efforts fail: poor communication.

Whether the change is planned and initiated, or externally created and therefore reactive, it's critical to engage your people in what it is, why it is happening, what the effect of it is likely to be on stakeholders, and WHAT PEOPLE SHOULD DO because of it. It's a truism to say that between 1/3 and 2/3 of CHANGE EFFORTS FAIL, and that the number one reason for that failure is POOR COMMUNICATION.

Some tips for engaging people in change:

→ ENGAGE THE PEOPLE AFFECTED BY THE CHANGE in helping to plan how to manage it and communicate about it – the best way to take people with you is to give them a role in shaping the change.

→ UNDERSTAND HOW CHANGE TENDS TO UNFOLD – Google "the change curve"; in essence, after raised emotions and expectations, there is a valley of despair, before things look up. There are also emotional phases people go through, e.g. Shock, Anger, Denial, Acceptance or any of a number of models.

Change should be done WITH, not TO people.

→ BE HONEST AND STRAIGHTFORWARD – when you don't know the answer to a question or are still working on solutions, communicate about it. Otherwise people will make up their own stories to improve upon your silence.

→ PLANS ARE FINE, BUT PLANNING IS PRICELESS – plan scenarios, mitigate risk. At least you'll know what direction you are meant to be going in. And if it happens to require a detour, you've still got a map.

DEPARTURE EXPERIENCE

Usually, people meet the challenges of their role, and after a while our person might start to think they need to move up, move over or move out. They seek to get what they need from their employment relationship by DOING SOMETHING DIFFERENT.

Sometimes, that means making sure you have in place the right career paths and development approaches, so people can be offered their next challenge within your organisation.

Sometimes, whether through reasons in your control or not, the person needs to move on to another challenge inside or outside your organisation.

Former employees = consumers, customers, sources of business and employee referral, and possibly future employees.

In either case, we have the opportunity to help ensure that the person remains MORE ENGAGED AND PRODUCTIVE during this period. We must also ensure that we are managing the process in such a way that every person who leaves becomes an advocate for us – or at least not a detractor. Firing people by text message doesn't tend to endear people to you or your brand in anyone's eyes.

Alumni programmes are one way leading organisations ensure that, at least for some employee categories, you create an ongoing connection with your leavers. It's never been easier, thanks to social media.

→ FIRST, they may recommend your company as a service provider, as a client or as an employer.

→ SECOND, they may come back to work for you again some day if you play your cards right.

→ AND THIRD, if you really sock it to them with a firm kick in the ass as they head out the door, they'll probably say terrible things (THAT MAY BE TRUE) about you and your brand. And that's not good. A good reputation is a hard thing to build and an easy thing to tarnish.

What are you saying?

Who are you saying it to?

Why does it matter to the business?

Who else is speaking to them at the same time?

Why should they care?

7. THE THREE Ms

There are as many techniques, theories, tips and tricks as there are books in the business section. Maybe even more. There's no way we can cover even a fraction of them.

BUT THAT'S NOT IMPORTANT. What is important is that whatever, whenever and however you choose to communicate and engage with your people, you are always, ALWAYS focussed on the Three Ms. Get these right and they are your passport to a brighter place:

→ MESSAGES – you should know what you want to say, and how you want to say it. Before you say it.

→ MEDIA – you should use the best possible approaches for your audience. Not for you. For your AUDIENCE.

→ MEASUREMENT – you should try to determine how well your engagement and communication is supporting what you are trying to achieve. If you aren't measuring something relevant to strategy or the bottom line, why are you measuring it?

Finally, most employee communication programmes benefit dramatically from involving those affected by it in their creation.

This is often called "co-development" or "co-creation" and the idea has been around since the '80s. It's pretty simple and at the heart of so-called kaizen, lean and other common-sense strategies: INVOLVE THE PEOPLE CLOSEST TO THE ACTIVITY IN SHAPING IT.

It's the difference between a bunch of suits in a room developing a strategy, and a cross-section of key stakeholders from top to bottom (including, if need be, external parties) in the design of the programme.

MESSAGES

CLEAR, CONSISTENT, CREDIBLE messages are essential for successful communication.

People don't really trust media spin and hype anymore, so you'd better be AUTHENTIC while you're at it.

Your messages should, whenever and wherever possible, be able to draw that red thread or line of sight to your core idea(s) – whether that's driven by brand, strategy, vision, values, or whatever.

The benefit of this is that you will always know why you are saying and doing things, and how to say and do them. You can tell it's going wrong when people are being bombarded

Three messages (plus or minus two).

with a wild and varied mix of messages and information from all corners of the organisation.

INFORMATION OVERLOAD and INFORMATION FATIGUE SYNDROME are real life phenomena both inside and outside the corporate environment. It causes stress and anxiety, and reduces people's cognitive abilities. It's a scientific fact that people can only really track three (+/- two) messages at a time.

In a perfect world, you could get away with a single overall core message, supported by three key messages, and a range of clear and compelling proof points or reasons to believe proving them. Of course, life can get more complicated, but the principle is the same; stick to your core truths and key messages. For example:

WE BELIEVE GOOD, FRESH FOOD IS BETTER.

|

GOOD, FRESH FOOD IS HEALTHIER

IT'S BETTER FOR OUR BUSINESS, OUR COMMUNITIES AND EMPLOYEES

EVERYTHING WE DO IS FOCUSSED ON THIS BELIEF

You know, you could probably map any HR, change, marketing, vision or values campaign back to this set of messages.

Don't select a channel or an approach because you can or because it exists.

Select it because it is the approach or channel that your audience trusts, uses and resonates with.

MEDIA

Ask an ad agency what the solution to your communication and engagement challenge is and guess what? It's an ad. (Low production value, user-generated look will incur additional fees.)

Ask an IT company, and guess what? It's a new system. (Wikified with blog functionality available at additional cost.)

Ask an HR professional, and it's about a human capital solution. (Applicant tracking system and destination career pipeline management will take a bit longer to implement.)

Ask an events company, and it's about a face-to-face experience extravaganza. (Dancing bears and smoke machines are extra). And so on.

Different people take in information in different ways. So use more than one channel, if you can. Make it interactive. Have your audience co-create the solution with you – it usually turns out better. People have greater ownership in things they had a hand in creating.

Another thought – the 22-year old founder of Facebook, recently said that "THE OTHER GUYS THINK THE PURPOSE OF COMMUNICATION IS TO GET INFORMATION. WE THINK THE PURPOSE OF INFORMATION IS TO GET COMMUNICATION."

Media planning is hard. But not planning makes it a lot harder. In my experience, INTENT usually counts more than TECHNIQUE.

Ultimately, if your measurement can't be tracked back to the top line, bottom line or at least a specific organisational outcome... Try again.

MEASUREMENT

Measuring the effectiveness of your communication and engagement efforts is important, and rightly so.

We need to know whether what we're doing is making any difference, because if it isn't, we need to do something else. There are numerous approaches to deciding what to measure, why to measure it, how to measure it and what success measures you want to aim for.

Quantitative measures give you hard data to work with. Executives and communicators tend to like statistics – WHAT GETS MANAGED GETS MEASURED. Or was it the other way around?

For attraction, recruitment and retention, good measures are quality of applicants, successful applications vs. number of applications received, cost per hire, employee turnover, etc.

For employee engagement, a pretty robust approach is to measure a number of things like how well people understand your brand and what they should do to deliver it; whether they'd recommend you as an employer or as a provider of products and services; whether they plan to (or would like to) still be working with you in a year's time. Then divide the data into quartiles and compare parts of the business with good performance and those with poor performance. Usually your engagement scores will correlate.

Then you can argue with your statistician about whether it's cause or effect.

Qualitative measures have re-emerged as a credible approach – focus groups, workshops, employee panels and so on are a great way to keep tabs on the pulse of the organisation and its people "hot spots."

The important thing is to know what influence you want to have on people's attitudes and behaviours, and then be able to see how you're doing.

8. DEFINITION OF TERMS

Most of the terms in this book should be pretty clear, but just in case, here's what I mean when I say...

ATTRACTION – getting the right people to want to come to work for you and not your competitors.

BRAND – the sum total of what and how people think and feel about your organisation, its people, and its products and services. Typically a significant intangible financial asset, but seldom managed like one. It's what they say it is, not what you say it is.

BRAND ENGAGEMENT – broadly, how connected people feel to your brand. In this context, brand engagement is about how well your employees and other stakeholders are connected to, and prepared to go the extra mile, for your products and services.

EMPLOYER BRAND – your reputation as an employer amongst potential and existing employees and other stakeholders. Again, it's what they say it is, not what you say it is.

EMPLOYEE JOURNEY — whether it's broken down into two stages or twelve, there is a well-embedded concept that breaks down the experience into touch points. In broad terms, thinking through how your engagement effort applies to people at each of the following stages of the employee journey can provide great insight into who needs to be involved, the potential ROI and benefits to the business, the best media and engagement techniques to apply, and what other actions need to be taken:

→ BRAND — a person knows something about your organisation, or learns about it, through a variety of touch points. These may include your consumer/corporate brand, product and service experience, word of mouth, recruitment advertising, or online experience.

→ EMPLOYER BRAND — at some stage, the person considers your organisation as a place where they might like to work. They seek information about your organisation — again from a range of sources, most of which your organisation has no control over whatsoever.

→ ATTRACTION & RECRUITMENT – the person decides to find out more about you, and to seek a job offer from your organisation. They experience your attraction and recruitment process and decide to join you or not join you.

→ ON-BOARDING AND INDUCTION – the person is inducted into the organisation and experiences "on-boarding".

→ FIRST 90 DAYS – the person experiences their initial time with your organisation, including initial perceptions, setting of initial goals, objectives and expectations, and forms a picture as to whether what you offered is what they receive.

→ ENGAGEMENT – the person continues to develop in their role (or not), and at various stages, they consider looking for a different role or challenge – with your organisation or with another organisation. Or, the organisation considers finding a different role for the person with itself or another organisation!

→ DEPARTURE EXPERIENCE – the person leaves employment with your organisation and may (or may not) consider rejoining at another stage, continuing to advocate your organisation as an employer, its products and services.

EMPLOYEE VALUE PROPOSITION – what you say and do to show what you offer as an employer, and what people can expect of an employment relationship with you.

ENGAGEMENT – employee engagement is broadly how much people care about, and are willing to do something extra for their career, their company, their colleagues, their communities and their customers. When it's working well, therefore, employee engagement is a good thing for everyone on your stakeholder list. Employee engagement delivers both commercial and cultural benefits to the organisation, and personal and professional benefits to the stakeholders involved.

INSANITY – doing the same thing but expecting different results. Often prevalent in employee communications. Alternatively, "If you always do what you've always done, you'll always get what you've always got!"

RETURN ON INVESTMENT/RETURN ON INVOLVEMENT (ROI) – getting more out than you would if you put your money in the bank or invested in something else (or if you want to calculate it, let us know your current discount rate).

→ ENGAGEMENT BUILDS SHAREHOLDER VALUE – smart companies understand that how they attract, engage and retain their people has as much impact on their business performance as their R&D, products and services, and marketing communications. Companies that do it well outperform those who don't.

→ ENGAGEMENT BUILDS BRAND EQUITY – your brand and intangible assets represent 40 to 70 percent of the total value of your organisation on your Finance Director's balance sheet. People make or break your reputation. And people are your greatest asset (according to your annual report). So it makes sense to manage your reputation, as a business and as an employer, like the important financial asset it is. It's no longer just about recruitment marketing and advertising either. It's just as much about marketing, advertising, PR, HR and internal communications.

→ ENGAGEMENT ENHANCES PRODUCTIVITY – there are always going to be employees who go the extra mile, and those who don't. The trick is to have as many of the good ones as possible. People don't join a company with the intention of "not being engaged." If you invest in making sure people have the awareness, attitude and tools to contribute, people will be more productive. They will contribute more, and the good ones will stay longer. Make sure your employer brand, employer value proposition – whatever you want to call it – is working hard as a business asset. It's critical to ensuring that you get the right people, that they get productive quickly, and that you don't have to go through the process of hiring them all over again.

→ ENGAGEMENT IMPROVES TALENT ATTRACTION & RETENTION – the simple act of making the effort to engage and give people a voice is often enough to make a difference, even to cynics. What's more is that your employees can act as a key channel to market for your reputation as a business and as an employer. It's not just about being nice – it's about cost saving and improved productivity. You can reduce recruitment advertising costs as well as agency fees if people become employer brand ambassadors.

→ ENGAGEMENT AFFECTS CUSTOMER ATTRACTION & RETENTION —
Organisations invest heavily in their infrastructures,
developing products and services, sales and marketing,
supply chain and getting their products and services to
markets at the price that will yield them the most profit.
You can get all of that right and still lose customers and
market share. The truth is that for nearly all products and
services, even if your performance and pricing are perfect,
poor service and interaction with your people – sales forces,
procurement people, customer facing, client facing and
service staff – is where your reputation is made or broken.
Customers are willing to forgive a lot if your people treat
them well.

STAKEHOLDERS – depending on your objectives, your stakeholders
may not be limited to employees of your organisation. Often,
engagement efforts need to take into account other stakeholders
who may be affected by changes in the way people inside your
organisation think and behave. These can include:

→ YOUR ORGANISATION – senior executives, leaders, business and
people managers, employees and contractors (and their families
and friends), former employees, future (potential) employees.

→ OTHER ORGANISATIONS – outsourced functions (HR, IT, etc.), suppliers, partners, regulators and government and related bodies.

→ THE BROADER COMMUNITY – the investment community, shareholders/investors, environmental and corporate responsibility interests.

→ YOUR CUSTOMERS, CONSUMERS OR CLIENTS – past, present and future.

→ YOUR COMPETITORS – direct "traditional" business competitors, non-traditional and indirect competitors, competitors for talent.

9. AFTERWORD

We went very fast and didn't have the time to take in all the sights. Many of the finer details and considerations were left, perhaps unconscious, in the dust cloud behind us. Just because the details aren't in this book doesn't mean they don't exist (gasp!).

Employee communication is serious business, but it's easy to take it all way too seriously. We aren't saving lives or solving the energy challenge (although many of our employers or clients might well be). Remember, as challenging as it is, all of this stuff can and should be really fun.

Just the same, I really believe most of us involved in employee communications have lost sight of the bigger picture. We tend to go around speaking at conferences as experts on little corners of it, from social media to writing for the web to intranets to cultural communications to executive coaching to photography. We've lost sight of how these things fit together, and if we want to stay relevant we need to start thinking and acting differently. There's a small group of us who have already started. Feel free to get in touch and join it, because this cool new playground is much bigger and better equipped than the one you might be used to.

Special thanks to DAN GRAY, who liked this book so much he went and wrote his own, and hence we gave birth to the 55-MINUTE GUIDE series. And, of course, a tip o' the hat to my colleagues and clients over the years. Most of the things I say in here I probably stole from you.

Some recommended sites and reading in no particular order:

GALLUP MANAGEMENT JOURNAL — WWW.GMJ.COM

SIMPLY COMMUNICATE — WWW.SIMPLY-COMMUNICATE.COM

MELCRUM PUBLISHING — WWW.MELCRUM.COM

INTERNATIONAL ASSOCIATION OF BUSINESS COMMUNICATORS — WWW.IABC.COM

BRITISH ASSOCIATION OF COMMUNICATORS IN BUSINESS — WWW.CIB.COM

RAGAN PUBLISHING — WWW.RAGAN.COM

CHARTERED INSTITUTE OF PERSONNEL DEVELOPMENT — WWW.CIPD.COM

MY BLOG, DEATH TO INTERNAL MARKETING — WWW.KEVINKEOHANE.COM

LINKS FROM MY BLOG TO OTHER BLOGS — WWW.KEVINKEOHANE.COM

THE GOWER HANDBOOK OF INTERNAL COMMUNICATION — MARC WRIGHT (ED.)

ON BRAND — WALLY OLINS

THE WISDOM OF CROWDS — JAMES SUROWIECKI

SIMPLICITY — EDWARD DE BONO

ZAG, THE BRAND GAP, THE DESIGNFUL COMPANY — MARTY NEUMEIER

VALUE DISCIPLINES — MICHAEL TREACY & FRED WIERSEMA

ABOUT THE AUTHOR

KEVIN KEOHANE is a business consultant who specialises in organisational communication. He has spent more than 20 years in the field of brand and employee communication.

After an education at The University of Denver and Georgetown University, his career took him to Australasia and Scandinavia, after which KEVIN moved to London, UK, where he has made his home for more than 10 years. During this time he co-founded the INTRANET BENCHMARKING FORUM (IBF) as well as the UK USABILITY PROFESSIONALS' ASSOCIATION (UK UPA). He has sat on the UK board of the INTERNATIONAL ASSOCIATION OF BUSINESS COMMUNICATORS (IABC) and holds professional accreditation from that organisation. He is also a Fellow of the BRITISH ASSOCIATION OF COMMUNICATORS IN BUSINESS (CIB) and a FELLOW OF THE ROYAL SOCIETY FOR THE ARTS. [An admittedly odd list from someone who by and large wouldn't join any club that would have him as a member...]

His clients have included some of the world's leading organisations, from AMERICAN EXPRESS to BARCLAYS to BP to BT to COCA-COLA to GLAXOSMITHKLINE to HP to KPMG to ORANGE to SHELL to VODAFONE and beyond.

Currently, KEVIN leads the PUBLICIS GROUPE'S MS&L BRAND AND TALENT NETWORK, a unique global network-within-a-network of agencies specialising in employee communications from its London hub, SAS (WWW.SASDESIGN.CO.UK).

He is passionate about Triumph motorcycles and enjoys track days or long rideouts, in addition to a thrilling daily commute through Central London taking him past Parliament, Big Ben, Buckingham Palace and Hyde Park twice a day. In his spare time he's also a song-writer and bass player (www.brandviolet.com).

You can reach him at kevin@kevinkeohane.com, via the blog (kevinkeohane.wordpress.com) or on LinkedIn.

Far too many business books start with the false premise that offering meaningful insight requires exhaustive detail. They demand a huge investment from readers to wade through all the information provided and draw out what is relevant to them.

In a rapidly changing, time-starved world, it's an approach that's getting wronger and wronger. What CEOs and other busy business people desperately need is high-level strategic insight delivered in quick, simple, easy-to-digest packages.

Co-created by KEVIN KEOHANE and DAN GRAY, that's exactly what the 55-MINUTE GUIDES are designed to do. Instead of some 300-page pseudo-academic tome, they offer fresh perspectives and "must knows" on important topics that can be read from cover to cover in the course of a single morning's commute or a short plane ride.

In short, they are the antidote to most business books. A QUICK READ, not a long slog. Focused on BIG IDEAS, not technical detail. Promoting JOINED-UP THINKING, not functional bias. Written to EMPOWER THE READER, not to make the author look clever.

They're guided by the simple principle that INSIGHT GAINED PER MINUTE SPENT READING should be as high as possible. No fluff. No filler. No jargon. Just the things you REALLY need to know, written in plain English with clear and simple illustrations.

Lightning Source UK Ltd.
Milton Keynes UK
UKOW021319090212

186992UK00012B/72/P